MW01222875

This Notebook Belongs To:

Made in the USA
Monee, IL
29 November 2019

17586624R00069